Why are monkeys so flexible?

World Book
answers YOUR questions
- about -
wild animals

WORLD
BOOK

www.worldbook.com

The questions in this book came from curious kids just like you who want to make sense of the world. They wrote to us at World Book with nothing but a question and a dream that the question they've agonized over would finally be answered.

Some questions made us laugh. Others made us cry. And a few made us question absolutely everything we've ever known. No matter the responses they induced, all the questions were good questions.

There isn't a strict rule for what makes a question good. But asking any question means that you want to learn and to understand. And both of those things are very good.

Adults are always asking, "What did you learn at school today?" Instead, we think they should be asking, **"Did you ask a good question today?"**

Why are monkeys so flexible?

Yoga.

They especially like Tree Pose and Turtle Pose. They do not—and we mean not—like Cow Face Pose. There was an incident. Don't ask. Just kidding! Aside from yoga, monkeys are flexible because they are adapted for life in the trees. Some kinds spend almost their entire life in the trees of such places as Central and South America. Their long arms and legs help them move from tree to tree. They can grasp things—like branches—with their hands and feet. Monkeys with long tails use them to keep their balance. And, of course, their abdominal training from yoga is sure to keep them from wibble-wobbling.

How do flamingos get their pink feathers?

9

First, they slog through sparkly sludge.

Then they fly over the majestic, magenta marina right into a giant vat of pink potion. Whoa, we're letting our imagination get the best of us. Flamingos get their pink feathers from the food they eat: shrimplike creatures and blue-

green algae. The food is filled with a substance called carotenoid. That's the same kind of chemical in pumpkins, sweet potatoes, and carrots. But you'll have to settle for the giant vat of pink potion to achieve their radiant, rosy glow.

Do animals dream?

13

Yes!

When people dream about becoming president, or painting a picture, or—uh oh—arriving at school wearing nothing but *polka-dot underpants,* they are going through REM (rapid eye movement) sleep. People dream during this period of sleep. Many animals also go through REM. Therefore, they dream. This is especially true of mammals and birds.

Are dragons real?

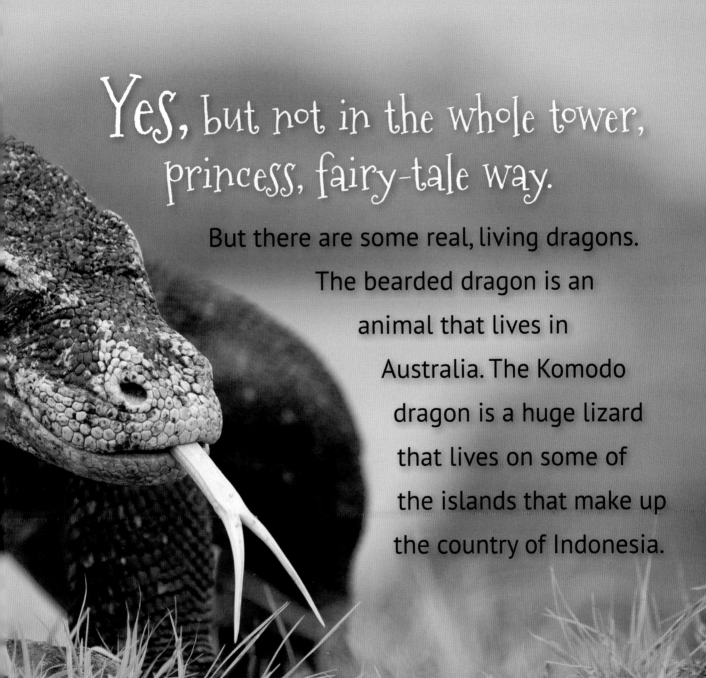

Yes, but not in the whole tower, princess, fairy-tale way.

But there are some real, living dragons. The bearded dragon is an animal that lives in Australia. The Komodo dragon is a huge lizard that lives on some of the islands that make up the country of Indonesia.

19

Can I
eat a wolf
for supper?

21

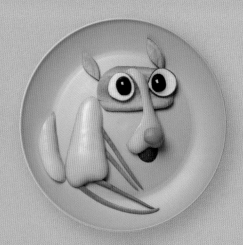

You could, but it would be a very, very bad idea for a number of reasons.

First, wolves are threatened or endangered in many regions. Second, wolves eat other animals, so the meat would be tough, stringy, and probably taste super-bad. Third, wolves eat huge amounts of substances that could make you super-sick. So, you'd be howling, all right. But not in a good, wolf-y way.

Why do snakes go underground?

Snakes go undergound when they get too hot.

They might test a few places: under bushes, logs, rocks, or water. But sometimes snakes go underground to *stay* warm. They do this in the really cold months. When it's fall or spring, they go above ground and get to wigglin' and slitherin' and warmin' up.

How do cheetahs communicate?

29

Through telephone.

But the connection can be pretty **spotty.** Ha! Get it? Spotty! Because they have spots! Although they are large cats, they can't roar like lions or tigers. They communicate vocally, but much more like a house cat. They even purr when they are content. When they want to protect their food or young from intruders, they hiss.

Is a blobfish made of jelly?

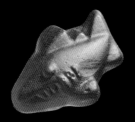

No, but it sure looks like it.

A blobfish looks like strawberry whipped cream or cherry pudding or a red velvet cake that *did not* turn out. It looks shapeless and...well, blobby, because its bones are soft and it doesn't have scales. The blobfish's loose skin has many folds that cover its fins. It does eat jelly-like things, though: sea slugs and worms.

What is the rarest animal?

We really wish we could tell you that.

But there are a lot of rare animals on Earth. Often, an animal is rare because the species is being wiped out. Some of the rarest endangered species are the Amur leopard, Sumatran orangutan, and black-eyed tree frog. Be sure to do things to protect the environment, so that more animals don't become rare.

Why are tigers soooooo big?

They want us to use six "O's" when we describe them.

Tigers are the top predators where they live. That means they hunt—and that they are very, very good at it. Tigers hunt such large animals as deer, pigs, and elephants. They need to be big to tackle their prey. Tigers also hunt alone, so they have to be strong to take down large prey by themselves.

How does a bear catch food?

45

With its bear hands.

Some bears wade into streams and catch fish with their front paws or strong jaws. Others search for acorns, pine seeds, berries, fruits, and nuts. Bears are sweet on honey, so they rip apart beehives.

Why are cheetahs so fast?

Why do alligators make a clicking noise,

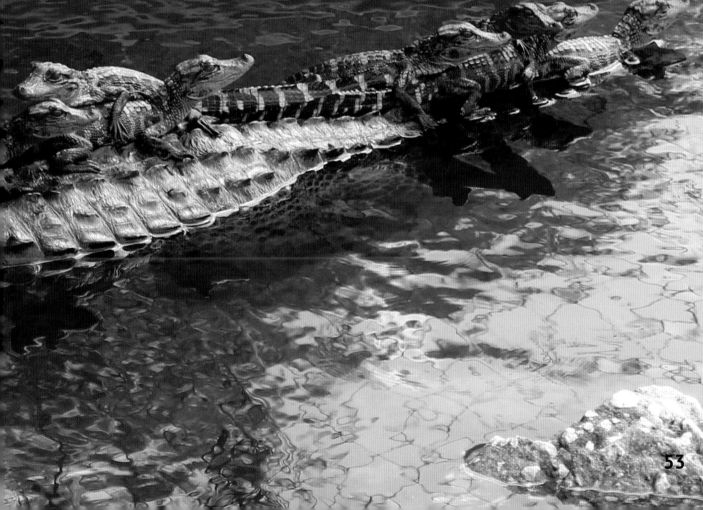

and why do they call their mama?

(click, click...click, click)

"I am hatching! I am about to see my first swamp—and my mama. She laid me and my brothers and sisters nine weeks ago. Now we want to see her. That's why I'm yelping. Now my mama can come scratch our eggs to open them. We'll be free. Hello, world!"

How do bats navigate and find food in the dark?

You don't normally eat with your ears, but bats do.

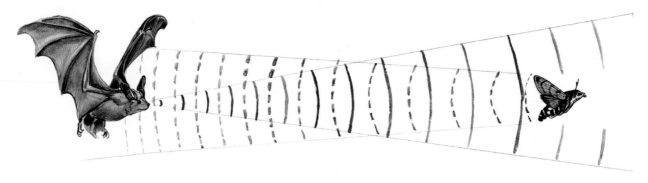

Sort of. Bats fly around in the dark and find food using an ability called *echolocation*. In echolocation, the animal makes a noise and listens for echoes from its surroundings. The echoes reveal details about the distance of objects in the animal's surroundings. This ability helps bats to "see" in the dark.

59

Can different species of animals

communicate
with each other?

We would say a flat out no, but that might get us in a sticky situation.

There is an African mammal called a ratel, also known as the honey badger. The ratel finds honey (its favorite food) by following a bird called the honey guide. The ratel hears the bird's call and follows it to a beehive. The ratel breaks open the hive—honey for all! But are the ratel and honey guide talking to each other? Probably not—it just seems like it. In general, different species of animals don't communicate with each other.

Hey! Got any honey left?

What do elephants eat?

You'd think that something that weighed 12,000 pounds (5,450 kilograms) would eat ice cream sundaes and cupcakes all day.

But, that isn't the case—although it would be fun. Elephants eat grass, water plants, and the leaves, roots, bark, branches, and fruit of trees and shrubs. They especially like bamboo, coconuts, and sugar cane. And they must eat a lot: a large adult elephant eats about 300 pounds (140 kilograms) of vegetation each day.

How far can an owl turn its head?

270 degrees.

Owls have fixed eye sockets, so their eyeballs can't rotate. This means that they have to stretch their necks to see things. They can even stretch so far to the right that they look left. Owls don't damage their blood vessels or cut off blood supply when they rotate. But you *definitely* would. Any owl would tell you that trying wasn't a wise idea.

Don't try this at home.

Why do giraffes have such long necks?

To make more giraffes with long necks.

One idea is that long necks developed in giraffes from competition. Male giraffes fight each other with their long necks. So, their long necks are basically weapons. The giraffe with the longer neck wins. And the female giraffes prefer the prize fighters. The female and male giraffe go on to have long-necked giraffe babies. Here's a surprising fact: Despite the length of its neck, a giraffe has only seven neck bones. That's the same number as humans!

75

Do emus bite?

Not usually.

Emus don't have teeth, but they have a pointed beak that could hurt if one of them pecked you with it. But most emus prefer to poke at fruits (peck), plants (peck), and insects (peck).

How do animals "laugh" when they think something is funny?

Why they laugh, of course.

Scientists have studied dogs, rats, chimpanzees, and other apes. They've found that those animals laugh when being tickled or playing. Their laughs, though, don't sound exactly like human laughs. They are breathier.

Why are chimpanzees bad with people?

Chimpanzees goofing around on television or in entertainment makes them appear friendly.

But, it's all fun and games until somebody gets hurt. And that somebody can be a person. Chimpanzees are wild animals that rarely interact with people in their natural habitat. Chimpanzees are very strong and can be dangerous to people, even if they don't mean to be. And, actually, people are bad with chimpanzees. They hunt the apes for food or capture them as household pets.

Why do lions have manes and tigers don't?

They're both cats, aren't they?

Is your Persian cat as vicious as a cheetah?

They are both cats, but that doesn't mean they look or act the same. The same is true with lions and tigers. Male lions are the only cats with manes. The mane makes the lion look even bigger and stronger than he is. It also protects him during fights, because the long, thick hair softens the blows of his foes. One possible reason that only male lions have manes is communication. A big mane shows others—especially females— that a male lion is healthy and strong.

What would you consider the smartest animal in the world?

You're going to like this answer.

It's human beings. You may be thinking, "I'm an animal?" Yes. Shocking, we know. Many other animals you may think of, such as chimpanzees, orangutans, and dolphins, are really smart. But humans have the most highly developed brain of any animal. With our brains, we create language and culture. And the richness and complexity of human culture makes us different from all other animals.

World Book, Inc.
180 North LaSalle Street
Suite 900
Chicago, Illinois 60601
USA

For information about other "Answer Me This, World Book" titles, as well as other World Book print and digital publications, please go to www.worldbook.com.

For information about other World Book publications, call 1-800-WORLDBK (967-5325).

For information about sales to schools and libraries, call 1-800-975-3250 (United States) or 1-800-837-5365 (Canada).

Library of Congress Cataloging-in-Publication Data for this volume has been applied for.

Answer Me This, World Book
ISBN: 978-0-7166-3821-6 (set, hc.)

Why are monkeys so flexible? World Book answers your questions about wild animals
ISBN: 978-0-7166-3830-8 (hc.)

Also available as:
ISBN: 978-0-7166-3840-7 (e-book)

Printed in China by RR Donnelley,
Guangdong Province
1st printing July 2019

J 590
WHY
420-0483

Staff

Editorial

Writers
Madeline King
Grace Guibert

Manager, New Content Development
Jeff De La Rosa

Manager, New Product Development
Nick Kilzer

Proofreader
Nathalie Strassheim

Manager, Contracts and Compliance
(Rights and Permissions)
Loranne K. Shields

Manager, Indexing Services
David Pofelski

Digital

Director, Digital Product
Development
Erika Meller

Digital Product Manager
Jonathan Wills

Graphics and Design

Senior Visual
Communications Designer
Melanie Bender

Media Editor
Rosalia Bledsoe

Manufacturing/Production

Manufacturing Manager
Anne Fritzinger

Production Specialist
Curley Hunter

Acknowledgments

Cover © Milan Zygmunt, Shutterstock; © Starikova Veronika, Shutterstock
3-33 © Shutterstock
34-35 © 4 Otogen/Shutterstock; Rachel Caauwe (licensed under CC BY-SA 3.0)
36-37 © Apple2499/Shutterstock; © Davdeka/Shutterstock; © Mark Brandon, Shutterstock; Vladlen Henríquez (licensed under CC BY-SA 2.5)
39-61 © Shutterstock
62-63 © Walter A. Weber, National Geographic/Getty Images; © Vishnevskiy Vasily, Shutterstock
64-95 © Shutterstock